STORM CHASERS

THE WILD AND VIOLENT SKIES OF KANSAS

CHRISTOPHER COLLURA

AMERICA
THROUGH TIME®
ADDING COLOR TO AMERICAN HISTORY

America Through Time is an imprint of Fonthill Media LLC
www.through-time.com
office@through-time.com

Published by Arcadia Publishing by arrangement with Fonthill Media LLC
For all general information, please contact Arcadia Publishing:
Telephone: 843-853-2070
Fax: 843-853-0044
E-mail: sales@arcadiapublishing.com
For customer service and orders:
Toll-Free 1-888-313-2665

www.arcadiapublishing.com

First published 2020

ISBN 978-1-63499-216-9

Typeset in Trade Gothic
Printed and bound in England

CONTENTS

About the Author 4

Introduction 5

1 Landscapes 7

2 Hail 16

3 Storm Structure 22

4 Tornadoes 48

5 Lightning 71

6 Sky and Atmosphere 79

7 Flooding and Damage 87

8 People and Storm Chasers 92

ABOUT THE AUTHOR

Christopher Collura has been actively pursuing severe weather before he even had a driver's license in the mid- to late 1980s. He began chasing storms in 1986 and has purposely been in nearly fifty tropical storms and hurricanes since late 1987. Since 1999, he has been logging countless miles each year chasing tornadoes in the Central USA, better known as "Tornado Alley." He has experienced tornadoes, tropical cyclones, hailstorms, wind, snowstorms, and more. More of his work can be found at www.sky-chaser.com.

INTRODUCTION

This book will take you through the adventures of the extreme weather and skies of Kansas through the eyes of a storm chaser who traveled there every year since the end of the twentieth century. Stunning landscapes, impressive cloud formations, strong winds, giant hail, flooding, and tornadoes were all encountered on his storm chasing endeavors and photography in this amazing state. Storm chasing in such areas can include exploring the beautiful landscape while passing the time, or waiting for storms to develop. When storms strike, storm chasers are often faced with their dangerous, yet beautiful aspects. Although beautiful, and like animals in many ways, severe storms can be deadly. The holy grail of storm chasing is witnessing a tornado or beautiful cloud-scape over open fields, displaying its power and bothering no one. Unfortunately, a town or farmstead gets hit by such a storm, and storm chasers often have to take the grim task of becoming first responders. See the effects of three air masses—dry air from the desert Southwest and Mexico, warm moist air from the Gulf of Mexico states and Caribbean to the southeast, and cold air from Canada and the Rocky Mountains to the north—all converging on a state that is in the center stage of "Tornado Alley" USA, causing some of the most interesting and bizarre weather unlike anywhere else on Earth.

A display of violent weather crosses the roadway about a mile in front of storm chaser Chris Collura near Geneseo, Kansas, during the late afternoon of April 14, 2012. This violent tornado tore from southwest to northeast across Rice County, and was on the ground for over 50 miles. Winds in the half-mile-wide funnel raged close to 200 MPH, flattening trees, completely destroying some homes, and even tearing the topsoil and grass out of the ground. Miraculously, no one was killed in this tornado, which was rated high-end EF-4 on a scale from EF-0 to EF-5.

1

LANDSCAPES

The state of Kansas offers amazing views and landscapes even during relatively tranquil weather. Massive wind turbines dot the landscape, providing renewable electrical power for much of the United States, while farming and livestock provide much of the nation's food supply. As a classic example of middle America, time seems to stand still in many areas, looking the same as it did a half a century ago. The combination of natural terrain, rural farmland, and an amazing sky makes Kansas a beautiful and interesting part of the Central United States.

Looking straight up at one of the massive wind turbines at the Gray County wind farm near Montezuma, Kansas, in May 2005. Each turbine is nearly twenty-two stories tall and can generate enough power for nearly 200 homes.

This is a view of the Gray County wind farm near Montezuma, Kansas, in May 2005. This is the largest wind turbine facility in Kansas and can generate 112 megawatts (or 33,000 homes usage) of electricity.

This is one of the eroded limestone buttes in Monument Rocks in Gove County, Kansas, in May 2005. A small area of fossilized landscape resembling the Desert Southwest rises from the green flat pastures.

One of the surprises of Kansas is the chalk formations of Monument Rocks in Gove County, Kansas. This is a beautiful formation of natural buttes of sandstone and limestone rising out of the otherwise dull prairieland in May 2005.

A familiar landscape in south-central Kansas between Dodge City and Wichita may look like this for many miles. Wheat gently waves in the wind with oil pump-jacks dotting the landscape during a warm day in May 2008.

Highway 183 stretches into the distance during "rush hour" south of LaCrosse, Kansas, late in a May afternoon in 2009, without a single car in sight. Hilly prairie lies on each side of the highway for miles.

As if they are completely oblivious to the impending threat of severe weather, these cows go about their daily lives on a pasture in northwestern Kansas in May of 2011. The Central United States is a major food source for millions of people.

The term "Central USA" cannot be more prominent here at this landmark! This subtle landmark, near Lebanon, Kansas, and in the middle of rural middle America, marks the exact center of the continental forty-eight United States.

After a day of storm chasing in late May 2012, this incredible sunset is being enjoyed near the Gray County wind turbine farm near Montezuma, Kansas. The dust in the air behind the dryline gives the setting sun and western sky these colors.

The relatively intact skeleton and hide of a long-passed cow leaves an impression in the grasslands of western Kansas in late May of 2012. Most likely a lightning strike caused this loss of this head of cattle.

Many railways are still alive and well across middle America, and Kansas is no exception. One major railway, popular for train spotting, is the Union Pacific Railroad, like this portion between Pratt and Greensburg, Kansas.

The impression of a dead wolf is left in the ground near Osborne, Kansas, on a hot day in late May of 2013. Just the bones, teeth, and fur may remain untouched for many years.

ABOVE: Kansas is noted for its many crops, with corn being one of the biggest. In this picture, a cornfield stretches across a northern Kansas field in early June of 2017. Kansas lies within the "corn belt" of the central USA.

PREVIOUS PAGE:

ABOVE: Looking down into the "Big Well" in Greensburg, Kansas. Since 1887, this is one of the largest hand-dug water wells, extending nearly eleven stories down. Greensburg was also destroyed by an EF-5 tornado in early May 2007.

BELOW: After a bout of severe storms and tornadoes in Texas and Oklahoma in mid-April of 2016, a blizzard affects western Kansas and eastern Colorado with heavy snow on the backside of the storm system. This picture was off Interstate 70 west of Goodland, Kansas, after the snowstorm.

2

HAIL

With the interaction of three major air masses across the Central United States, Kansas can be home to some of the largest hail on earth. As cold Canadian air spills southward over the warmer air from the Gulf of Mexico, powerful thunderstorms with violent updrafts, powerful enough to rip the wings off an airliner, can produce and keep ice aloft long enough so that it grows to the size of softballs, only to fall 8 miles back to earth and damage anything in its path.

Looking south near the Colorado border, a supercell storm erupts near Tribune, Kansas, in late May of 2005. The white streaks falling from the cloud base is large hail that will ultimately cover the ground like snow.

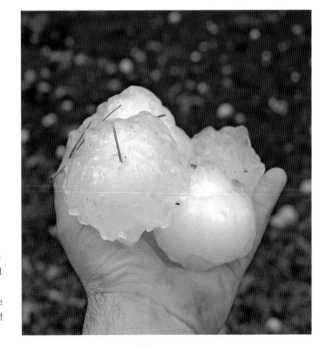

Gigantic hail stones, baseball sized or larger, clobber a small northeastern Kansas town near the Missouri border late in the day in early June 2009. Such giant hail stones are formed by powerful storm updrafts near 150 MPH and can total a car in less than four minutes! The name "gorilla hail" is given to such giant hail stones.

Extremely large hail, some as big as a grapefruit, covers the ground in a small northeastern Kansas town as a supercell crosses the Missouri River in early June of 2009. Hail this size can kill livestock and destroy crops.

While attempting to drive away from a powerful supercell between Pratt and Greensburg in Kansas in May 2008, baseball-sized hail falling from 30,000+ feet out of the storm anvil shattered the windshield of my chase vehicle (among dented metal and shattered plastic).

A menacing low cloud base pushes east of Scott City, Kansas, during an early evening in late May of 2010. The hail core to the right is tinted green as the late day sunlight is filtered by the tall storm clouds.

After large hail fell in northeastern Kansas late on a chase day in May 2010, we decided to break a stone in half, revealing this onion-like internal structure. Like rings in a tree, each layer is one trip up and down the storm updraft, at least 20,000 feet, until if grows too heavy and falls out of the storm.

Numerous quarter-sized hail stones were collected from the ground under an intense low precipitation supercell storm to the southwest of Goodland, Kansas, in late May of 2013. Despite being called "low precipitation" storms, these storms often produce large hail.

The scene behind a supercell storm in a western Kansas town often looks like this, with large hail accumulating as if a snowstorm occurred in the middle of late spring. Unlike snow, driving on hail is like driving on marbles.

Hail, some as large as tennis balls, covers the roadway behind a tornadic supercell storm near Medicine Lodge, Kansas, after dusk in early April 2015. This is more hazardous than driving on snow as these balls of ice act like driving on marbles.

The intense core of a supercell moving out of eastern Colorado towards Sharon Springs, Kansas, pushes rapidly east and drops copious amounts of golf-ball sized hail with a rainbow during an evening in late June of 2019.

3

STORM STRUCTURE

The exceptional power of the violent storms of "Tornado Alley" can be both beautiful, terrifying, and even surrealistic at the same time. Warm air rising into regions of cooler air and stronger winds at higher altitudes produces powerful thunderstorms, called "supercells." These rotating storms are very rare compared to other types of thunderstorms, but are common during the severe weather season in Kansas and the Central United States. The combination of wind shear, rapidly rising air, rotation, and downdrafts can cause cloud formations and storm structure unlike anywhere else on Earth.

A classic supercell—where the precipitation core is displaced downwind of the main updraft, in this case to the right—churns over Russell County near Hays, Kansas, late in the day in May 2004. Looking west, we are watching the low rotating portion of the storm to see if any tornadoes form.

This is a low precipitation supercell storm (a rotating storm that produces little visible rain) near Studley, Kansas, in May of 2003. The storm was weakening and the jet stream aloft it was literally tearing the storm apart via wind shear, but there was not enough instability to overcome it.

An intensifying low precipitation supercell storm approaches western Kansas from northeastern Colorado near Goodland in late May of 2004. Large hail to baseball sized is most likely falling to the lower right in this picture.

A classic supercell thunderstorm erupts near Bellview, Kansas, late in the day in May 2004. This storm produced multiple tornadoes. Looking west, the heavy precipitation is falling to the right and any tornadoes will develop from the "wall cloud" in the center.

A small tornado, denoted by the dust swirl beneath a menacing supercell cloud base, appears in northwestern Kansas in May 2005. Such tornadoes are often called "landspouts" and occur in dry air under storms where a visible funnel is absent under the cloud base.

ABOVE: This is a view into the "notch" of a high-precipitation supercell, where rain and hail wraps around much of the storm's circulation in late May of 2008 in Gove County, Kansas. The low clouds in the foreground and background are rapidly moving in opposite directions.

PREVIOUS PAGE:

ABOVE: A beautiful presentation of colors occurs as a severe thunderstorm lumbers eastward towards Osborne, Kansas, at dusk in late May 2005. This is the "gust front" or leading edge of the storm's outflow winds, approaching 80 MPH.

BELOW: A developing tornado, with rapid rotation, approaches the Missouri River in northeastern Kansas in late May of 2004. This rotating cloud, called a wall cloud, will eventually produce multiple tornadoes in western Missouri.

ABOVE: The powerful rear-flank downdraft is a wind that sinks behind a developing tornado. Here such a wind is trying to make a supercell wall cloud "spin up," looking northwest from Castle Rock Road in Gove County, Kansas, in late May of 2008.

NEXT PAGE:

ABOVE: While headed southwest into north-central Kansas near Tipton in late May of 2008, this unworldly looking supercell looms over the horizon in a "high risk" area for tornadoes. The rapid rotation of the storm gives it a flying-saucer-like appearance.

BELOW: A small area of rotation develops over northeastern Kansas near Summerville late in the day in May of 2012. This storm did not produce a tornado, but very large hail that damaged vehicles in the area.

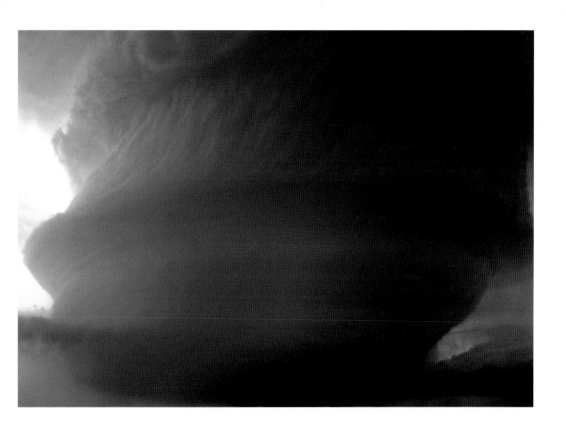

A high-based storm, with a storm chasing tour group in the foreground, develops in extreme northwestern Kansas during the early evening in June of 2015. This storm will remain over open country and produce strong winds and large hail.

This is a view of the gust front of an outflow-dominant storm northeast of Kingman, Kansas, during the afternoon on a mid-May day in 2010. The leading edge of cold storm outflow produces this low and "shelf cloud" formation.

A wall cloud, which is a lowered thunderstorm base caused by moisture convergence, hangs over rural areas of Leoti, Kansas, with a weakening supercell in late May of 2010. These low cloud bases sometimes, but not always, indicate tornado formation.

A weak tornado, with swirling dust, develops with a rotating cloud base as a supercell storm pushes out of far northeastern Colorado and into the flat terrain of Kansas northwest of Goodland during a late May afternoon in 2010.

A line segment, which is a line of severe thunderstorms packing 80 MPH winds, pushes nearly unnoticed by many across the hilly rural farmlands of extreme northern Kansas during the early evening in late May 2010.

Although looking rather threatening, this is just a marginally severe thunderstorm, with 60 MPH winds and nickel-sized hail, pushing across northern Kansas during the late morning in May of 2012. The more severe storms are yet to come later in the afternoon.

A low precipitation and low topped supercell storm develops along a stalled cold front near LaCrosse, Kansas, in early April of 2013. The sun is setting behind the storm, providing the back lightning and colors in this picture.

A low precipitation storm develops along a sharp cold front in early April 2013 west of Goodland, Kansas. Here the temperature is around 80 degrees, and in twenty-four hours it will be 15 degrees with ice and snow!

ABOVE: A powerful tornadic supercell storm develops in the afternoon near Wichita, Kansas, in mid- to late May 2013. The backside of this storm shows the storm updraft and "anvil" shaped crown extending to at least 50,000 feet.

PREVIOUS PAGE:

ABOVE: A powerful updraft and rock-hard "cauliflower" appearance is visible on this low precipitation supercell storm west of Goodland, Kansas, in early April 2013. This storm is developing along an extreme Canadian cold front, with snow and frigid temperatures to follow.

BELOW: Late-day view of a supercell storm developing ahead of a frigid Canadian air mass in western Kansas in early April 2013. In twenty-four hours, the associated cold front will cause the temperature to drop nearly 65 degrees.

Like a scene from an alien invasion movie, the leading edge of a low precipitation supercell storm, resembling a "flying saucer," creeps along the Kansas/Nebraska border north of Osborne in late May 2013. The strong wind shear and powerful rotation give the cloud this surrealistic appearance.

A beautiful and surrealistic flying-saucer-like formation passes over the northern Kansas/Nebraska border in late May of 2013. This low precipitation supercell had these crazy cloud striations and produced hail up to tennis ball sized.

A high based low precipitation supercell pushes eastward along Interstate 70 between Goodland, Kansas, and the Colorado border in May of 2014. The storm produced strong winds and large hail to golf ball sized.

Beautiful cloud striations and storm structure of a low precipitation supercell storm west of Goodland, Kansas, after dusk in May of 2014. These high-base storms are both pretty and destructive, producing high winds and very large hail.

ABOVE: A lowering of the dark updraft base called a wall cloud, rotates and forms a large funnel with a supercell storm northwest of a rural intersection in extreme northwestern Kansas in June of 2015.

PREVIOUS PAGE:

ABOVE: An elevated supercell storm moves out of extreme northeastern Kansas before noon in mid-June of 2014. The cool downdraft creates the low roll cloud beneath the storm, which also produced hail as large as softballs.

BELOW: The wet rear-flank downdraft of a high precipitation supercell moves across Grainfield, Kansas, during a storm chase in late April of 2015. These so called "HP storms" are often completely wrapped with rain and hail, obscuring any tornadoes inside.

Powerful outflow winds, sometimes called a *derecho*, which simply means "straight ahead" in Spanish, kick up dust in a storm near Liberal, Kansas, in May 2001. Straight line winds near 100 MPH can cause the same damage as a tornado.

This is a view of a striated shelf cloud, marking the leading edge of powerful straight line (outflow) winds as high as 100 MPH, associated with a *derecho* in southwest Kansas in late May of 2001.

A menacing dark wall of clouds, called a shelf cloud, marks the leading edge of the cold outflow air of a severe storm over extreme western Kansas. Behind this "gust front," strong winds and large hail are present.

The southern end of a line segment of severe thunderstorms pushes out of Colorado and into extreme northwestern Kansas in early May of 2016. Storms in these areas rotate hard, producing incredible structure like this, and sometimes tornadoes.

A formerly tornadic classic supercell moves away from Dodge City towards Jetmore, Kansas, in late May 2016. This storm stopped producing tornadoes, but now will produce extreme hail nearly the size of coconuts as storms evolve into clusters of supercells.

The start of a long string of at least nine tornadoes from a single cyclic supercell may look no more than a low rotating cloud base as shown here north of Mineola, Kansas, in late May of 2016.

A highly sheared and small low-precipitation supercell spins along a dry-line bulge near El Dorado, Kansas, in late May of 2016. This structure resembles a "barber pole" and is called such by storm chasers.

ABOVE: The cold outflow from a severe thunderstorm can travel for many miles, forming a gust front and "arcus" cloud far from the original storm. This was such a gust front near Emporia, Kansas, in late May of 2016.

NEXT PAGE:

ABOVE: An intense supercell pushes out of extreme eastern Colorado and into northwestern Kansas along Interstate 70 west of Goodland in late May of 2017. The storm evolved to a bow segment, with this beautiful multi-tiered shelf cloud.

BELOW: A distant left split of a supercell storm extends to high altitude and is radically tilted by the strong winds aloft with a windmill silhouette in the foreground near Vermillion, Kansas, late in the day in June of 2019.

ABOVE: The leading edge of a damaging *derecho* of destructive straight-line winds as high as 100 MPH approaches the small town of Sharon Springs, Kansas, along Highway 40 in late June 2019. Note the multi-tiered shelf cloud ahead of the supercell.

NEXT PAGE:

ABOVE: A beautiful and striated low precipitation supercell passes near Vermillion, Kansas, near dusk in late June of 2019. This storm will eventually shrink until it is no more than a tiny cloud, in a process called "down-scaling."

BELOW: A supercell storm intensifies over far eastern Colorado and moves into the high plains of western Kansas in late June of 2019. Here the storm is evolving into a bow segment, with 100 MPH winds, in a process called "up-scaling."

4

TORNADOES

The state of Kansas lies in a section of the Central United States called "Tornado Alley." The severe weather season is mainly in late spring, where three different air masses interact. The combination of this and strong jet stream winds at great heights above the earth cause rotating thunderstorms called "supercells" to erupt over Kansas more than anywhere else on Earth. Occasionally this rotation becomes strong enough to produce a violently rotating column of air (the "tornado") extending down from the parent supercell storm, with winds anywhere from 40 to nearly 320 miles per hour. Tornadoes are rated from EF-0 to EF-5, with "5" being the strongest, all of which have wrecked havoc across the state of Kansas.

This is a powerful rotating vortex within strong outflow in a severe *derecho* near Liberal, Kansas, in late May of 2001. These small tornado-like rotations, common along storm gust fronts, are known as "gustnadoes."

Tornado formation, or technically "tornado-genesis," occurring with a powerful classic supercell storm approaching Interstate 70 near Grinnell, Kansas, in late May of 2008. Here a funnel and ground circulation is developing, and will form a large tornado north of town.

A long and sinuous tornado, known as a "rope tornado," stretches across most of the western sky north of Grinnell, Kansas, on a late May day in 2008. This tornado fortunately remained over open farmland, damaging only crops.

A massive tornado at close range, over a mile wide, appears as a wall of fast-moving, ground-scraping clouds north of Quinter, Kansas, in late May 2008. Looking closely, the smaller sub-vortices making up the large tornado can be seen.

This is a developing tornado under a powerful supercell storm near Tipton, Kansas, during a tornado outbreak in late May of 2008. This tornado will move northeast, causing EF-3 damage in the small town of Jewell, packing 160 MPH winds.

Wide angle of a violent supercell storm near Glen Elder reservoir in Kansas in late May of 2008. A tornado, with 160 MPH winds, is occurring under the flying-saucer-like structure in this picture. The same tornado will also cause extensive damage in Jewell.

ABOVE: A classic supercell storm looms over the horizon, with a developing tornado dangling from its rain-free base, during a tornado outbreak in central Kansas near Rush County in mid-April of 2012.

PREVIOUS PAGE:

ABOVE: A severe storm crosses from extreme eastern Colorado and into Kansas, near Tribune, during the afternoon in late May 2010. The distinct view of a tornado becomes apparent on the northeastern horizon, appearing white due to the light angle.

BELOW: Tornado "genesis," meaning the formation of a tornado, is marked by a funnel and rapidly rotating wall cloud on the southwestern side of a supercell storm to the northwest of Tribune, Kansas, in late May of 2010.

ABOVE: A small but powerful tornado snakes its way across the roadway looking west on a high-risk tornado outbreak day in mid-April of 2012 near Rush Center, Kansas.

NEXT PAGE:

ABOVE: A classic supercell storm pushes across the Kansas farmland near Rush Center during the afternoon of a high-risk tornado outbreak day in mid-April of 2012. This tornado fortunately missed any populated areas.

BELOW: A long-track tornado, with a history of damage and 200 MPH winds, continues to the northeast of Rice County, Kansas, during the afternoon of a high-risk tornado outbreak in mid-April of 2012.

A violent tornado rapidly develops to the southwest of Geneseo, Kansas, in Rice County during a mid-April afternoon in 2012. This tornado would cause EF-4 damage, with winds up to 200 MPH.

A violent tornado, with winds approaching 200 MPH and causing high-end EF-4 damage (on a scale from 1 to 5) ravages a farmstead to my north during a storm chase in Rice County, Kansas, in mid-April of 2012.

An elephant trunk shaped tornado emerges from the heavy precipitation of a supercell near Viola, Kansas, in late May of 2013. This is actually a smaller tornado rotating around a larger one that is hidden in the rain to the right.

A large, and nearly perfect, wedge tornado sits nearly stationary over a field near Bennington, Kansas, in late May of 2013. This tornado was rated EF-4, with winds at least 180 MPH, damaging trees, farm equipment, and killing cows.

ABOVE: A violent, but nearly stationary, wedge tornado churns over rural terrain near Bennington, Kansas, in May of 2013. Missing any towns, this EF-4 tornado killed some cattle and destroyed some farming equipment over the course of an hour.

PREVIOUS PAGE:

ABOVE: Tornado development, or tornado-genesis, occurring near Bennington, Kansas, on a late May afternoon in 2013. This will develop into a wedge tornado, wider than it is tall, and remain stationary over open farmland for nearly an hour.

BELOW: A classic tornadic supercell produces a large tornado near Bennington, Kansas, in late May of 2013. The incredible striated structure of the supercell can be seen, with a tornado beneath it that stayed on the ground for nearly and hour.

ABOVE: A "cinnamon bun" cloud formation occurs with a low precipitation supercell storm moving into extreme western Kansas near Kanorado in May of 2014. A weak and dusty tornado is also developing with this storm.

NEXT PAGE:

ABOVE: A powerful supercell storm develops to the southwest of Medicine Lodge, Kansas, in early April of 2015. A brief wedge tornado descends from the low cloud base looking southwest over open farmland, fortunately causing no major damage.

BELOW: The first of many tornadoes touches down to the north of Mineola, Kansas, on a developing violent supercell in late May of 2016. The two cars near the tornado are two storm chasers who were very close to the storm.

A cyclic supercell, where one tornado forms after another, even simultaneously, rages over open country to the southwest of Dodge City, Kansas, in late May of 2016. At least two tornadoes are on the ground at the same time.

An elephant trunk tornado develops east of a larger tornado to its west near Dodge City, Kansas, in late May of 2016. This one "cyclic" storm produced nearly nine tornadoes over the course of a few hours.

A "cyclic" supercell, with the first tornado to the left on-going, and a new one forming to the right, rages over open farmland southwest of Dodge City, Kansas, in late May of 2016, barely missing barns and grain bins.

A cyclic supercell storm, that is a tornadic supercell that produces multiple tornadoes, spawns multiple tornadoes simultaneously to the southwest of Dodge City, Kansas, in late May of 2016. Luckily this storm system passed west of town, sparing it from certain devastation.

ABOVE: A violently rotating wall cloud, and developing EF-3 multi-vortex tornado, skims past the western side of Dodge City, Kansas, in late May 2006. The storm barely missed the small city and spared it from major devastation.

NEXT PAGE:

ABOVE: A weakening rope tornado starts to disappear in the rain and hail to the left as a new mesocyclone develops, or "cycles," to the right, within a cyclic supercell north of Dodge City, Kansas, in May 2016.

BELOW: The first touchdown of a tornado late in the afternoon between Mineola and Dodge City, Kansas, in late May of 2016. This tornado is the first of nearly nine tornadoes produced by this cyclic supercell.

The first of many tornadoes produced by a storm southwest of Dodge City, Kansas, comes perilously close to two distant storm chase vehicles in late May of 2016. Fortunately, these tornadoes remained over open farmland and caused little damage.

Simultaneous tornadoes, one weakening to the left, and one intensifying to the right, descend from a cyclic supercell southwest of Jetmore, Kansas, in late May of 2016. The "cycling" is a new tornado forming ahead of the previous one in succession.

A final tornado, probably the ninth one in a "family" of tornadoes, descends from a cyclic supercell south of Jetmore, Kansas, well behind a stop sign in late May of 2016. If you were a storm chaser, I doubt you would stop!

A massive and violent tornado, with at least EF-4 winds near 200 MPH, slices north of Interstate 70 near Chapman, Kansas, during an early evening in late May 2016. This wedge tornado was on the ground at least 90 minutes!

Baseball-sized hail falls in the foreground of a ground-shaking mile-wide violent tornado, that lasted 90 minutes, near Chapman, Kansas, in late May 2016. The only creature on Interstate 70 is a turtle to the lower left.

A tornado, denoted by a ground circulation of dust under a visible funnel, develops over a wind turbine farm near Ellsworth, Kansas, during an afternoon on the first day of May in 2018.

A large and violent EF-4 tornado, with winds near 180 MPH, develops over an open field east of Tescott, Kansas, late on the first day of May in 2018. A farmhouse was later completely destroyed by this tornado.

A bunch of cows continue to graze and mingle on a ranch, in the foreground and nearly oblivious, as a powerful tornado touches down close behind them east of Tescott, Kansas, on the first day of May in 2018.

A tornado descends from a lengthy dark cloud base under a supercell storm near Kinsley, Kansas, in mid-June of 2019. The tornado is about five miles away from this bend in Highway 183 and weakened shortly after.

5

LIGHTNING

The wide-open skies and flat terrain of Kansas make it one of the most interesting places to see lightning. All thunderstorms can produce lightning, which forms from charge separations within the tall cumulonimbus clouds. Imagine a small static shock after walking across a carpet, but literally many millions of times that scale. Lightning can carry a voltage potential of hundreds of millions of volts, an a current of tens of thousands of amps, heating the air to five times the temperature of the sun's surface. The expansion of this super heated plasma creates a shock wave and the sound we call "thunder."

ABOVE: Smooth channel lightning, that is lightning that is not "forked" in appearance, strikes the ground in front of a developing tornado near Wakeeney, Kansas, in late May 2008. This lightning is positively charged (rarer than the more common negative lightning) due to down-drafts bringing the positively charged cloud layers, normally higher up, closer to the ground, and is often a pre-cursor to tornado genesis.

PREVIOUS PAGE:

ABOVE: Lightning forks in the sky during a severe storm near Tribune, Kansas, after dark in late May of 2005. The storm chasers and vehicles in the foreground are relatively safe from the deadly lightning strikes roughly 5 miles away.

BELOW: Twin lightning bolts pierce the sky beneath a high-precipitation supercell storm well after dark, north of a small town northwest of Emporia, Kansas, in June of 2007. Lightning is the greatest risk to storm chasers.

ABOVE: Lightning pierces the sky near Atwood, Kansas, after dark in late May of 2010. This is CG or "cloud to ground" lightning, the most dangerous to people in the strike zone.

NEXT PAGE:

ABOVE: A beautiful and distant supercell storm with frequent lightning illuminates the moonlit and starry skies north of Salina, Kansas, during the early nighttime hours in late May of 2012.

BELOW: An incredible display of lightning and mammatus, or breast shaped clouds, surrounds a powerful supercell storm as it crosses from Nebraska into northern Kansas after dark in late May of 2013. Extreme turbulence aloft sculpts the high cloud layers into such formations.

ABOVE: A cloud to ground, or CG lightning bolt, pierces the sky during the passage of a line of severe thunderstorms north of Wichita, Kansas, in early October of 2016. This type of lightning is the most dangerous to people.

PREVIOUS PAGE:

ABOVE: This is a view of a supercell storm on the southern portion of a line of storms west of Salina, Kansas, after dark in late May of 2013. Lightning provides illumination for the storm. The rotating portion of the storm is to the lower right.

BELOW: A low topped tornadic supercell rapidly moves northward into the distant night sky near Grinnell, Kansas, in early May 2015. The lightning illuminated storm glows brightly, even revealing a large tornado under the storm, just left of the center of the picture.

A large cloud-to-ground lightning strike illuminates an elevated severe thunderstorm just before midnight in extreme southwestern Kansas in late April of 2017. These high-based storms make for an impressive, but dangerous, display of lightning.

Intense, and close strike, of cloud-to-ground lightning in extreme southwestern Kansas from a storm moving out of Oklahoma during the evening in late May of 2018. Lightning like this poses the highest risk for storm chasers.

6

SKY AND ATMOSPHERE

Outside of any major storms and severe weather, the general appearance of the sky over Kansas can be a source of awe and wonder. Above the beautiful terrain and farmlands, the air currents high above Kansas, stirred by the jet stream, sun angles, and air mass interactions, can create intriguing cloud formations and sky colors unlike anything we see elsewhere.

ABOVE: A departing cold front, and the clash of warm and cold air, makes for these interesting cloud "swirls" looking east of Fort Scott, Kansas, late in the day in early October of 2009.

PREVIOUS PAGE:

ABOVE: A beautiful cloudscape and rainbow appears amidst heavy rains and large hail while looking eastward into extreme western Kansas in late May of 2005. The storm will produce large hail and flooding near Tribune, Kansas.

BELOW: Sometimes a flight over Kansas during a severe storm outbreak can offer a majestic view of cloud formations to those with a window seat. In this picture, thunderstorms tower near 60,000 feet, twice the altitude of the airliner, during early summer in 2006.

ABOVE: A fiery sky prevails to the west over a western Kansas town in late May of 2010. Both the upper level trough, weakening storms, and surface dry-line sculpt the high altitude clouds into such optical formations at dusk.

NEXT PAGE:

ABOVE: These are known as *mammatus* (Latin for "breast shaped") clouds streaming high above a small town in northern Kansas near the Nebraska border around sunset in late May 2010. Extreme turbulence aloft interacts with the jet stream at high altitudes forming these bizarre and beautiful clouds.

BELOW: The late afternoon sun and tall supercell clouds paint the sky into a picturesque set of colors when looking west out of western Kansas in early June of 2010. This area is also nearly 5,000 feet elevation, higher than many areas in the eastern United States.

When flying high over Kansas during a clear day, one may look down and see a pattern like this. These are center pivot circular irrigation farms that provide corn, wheat, alfalfa, and soybeans for much of the US population.

The atmospheric optics can present a beautiful scene, with crepuscular rays of sunlight peeking through the cloud layers during a late May afternoon in western Kansas while heading west along Interstate 70.

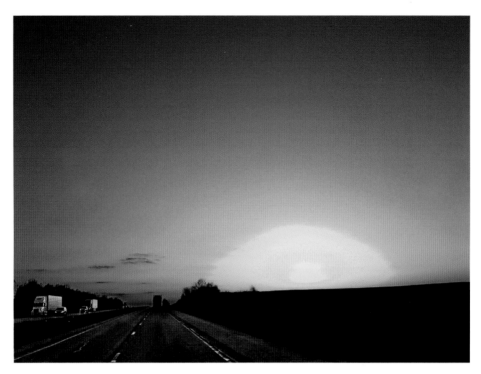

Sometimes after a day of severe storms and tornadoes, the "dry-line" pushes through. This is a front of dry air from the west, with clear skies. Behind this boundary, a sunset like this one in western Kansas can be enjoyed.

Dust gets kicked up and seriously reduces visibility while being overtaken by a strong gust front east of a severe thunderstorm in northwestern Kansas in early June of 2015. This dust plume is also called a "haboob."

A distant supercell storm looms over the horizon as a long roll cloud, driven by cool outflow and called an "arcus," pushes well ahead of the storm complex over a wheat field in southwestern Kansas in late May of 2017.

A beautiful field of high-level *mammatus*, or breast-shaped clouds, glows after dark over extreme northern Kansas and southern Nebraska after severe storms during an evening in late June 2019. These clouds are a threat only to airliners, with extreme turbulence.

7

FLOODING AND DAMAGE

The state of Kansas, as with many other places in the Central United States, is affected by anything from flooding to devastation due to severe weather. Heavy rain and melted hail can cause flash flooding, or turn a dry country road into a vehicle death-trap of deep mud from which no 4x4 can escape from. Tornadoes, hail, and strong winds can cause damage ranging from a tree knocked down to entire neighborhoods being wiped out. The people of Kansas are proud and strong, and occasionally have to be knowledgeable and accept the risks of living in this area prone to such severe weather.

Heavy rains can turn these dirt roads into deep mud that can trap even 4x4 vehicles. The only way to get out of this mess south of Quinter, Kansas, in May 2008 was to be pulled out by a tractor.

Shredded sheet metal, most likely from roofs or grain bins, lines the sides of a dirt road north of Quinter, Kansas, after a mile-wide tornado struck the area a day earlier in late May of 2008.

Twisted sheet metal, from a roof or grain bin, is wrapped around a shattered power pole stump in the wake of a large tornado near Quinter, Kansas, in late May 2008. The direction of the winds is evident in the way the debris is laid out and is important for tornado research.

The utter destruction of a small town after a violent tornado passes through is something that is both heartbreaking and terrifying. Buildings and lives remain torn apart after a devastating EF-5 tornado moved into Joplin, Missouri, from a storm near Independence, Kansas, in late May of 2011.

ABOVE: Severe flooding was a big problem all across the Central United States in May of 2019. In this picture, a roadway east of Abilene, Kansas, disappears into a flash flood area. There are also railroad tracks submerged beneath this new "lake" that was formerly a corn field.

PREVIOUS PAGE:

ABOVE: The sheer power of at least EF-4 tornado winds, approaching 200 MPH, are capable of stripping the bark off trees in the damage path. This denuded, and debarked, tree was after the passage of a violent tornado in Rice County near Geneseo, Kansas, in mid-April 2012.

BELOW: A farm becomes a lake after the passage of a high precipitation supercell, and nearly 10 inches of rain, in May of 2014 in extreme western Kansas. Note the white hail covering the landscape in the distance.

8

PEOPLE AND STORM CHASERS

During the severe weather season, both the people of Kansas and those visiting there must be aware of the dangers of extreme weather during the severe weather season. Storm chasers, ranging from amateurs to scientists, descend into Kansas and the nearby states to document the extreme weather each year. The local people of Kansas are highly aware and humbled by the threat of storms each year, and often proud that storm chasers can offer the services of watching the sky for any dangers, as well as helping with timely warnings and "ground truth" of storms.

A DOW truck, or "Doppler radar on wheels," passes along Highway 81 to the east of a tornado near Bennington, Kansas, in May of 2013. The inflow bands can be seen curving into the storm overhead.

Like many times before, here is a picture of myself gearing up for another western Kansas chase in May of 2016. The chase vehicle has everything I need to actively pursue severe weather.

ABOVE: Storm chasers and scientists, including the Doppler radar truck, park on the side of the road and collaborate in Greensburg, Kansas, before a storm chase day in early May of 2016.

PREVIOUS PAGE:

ABOVE: Hard working local farmers greet my group as we wait for storms to develop in a small town in far southwestern Kansas in May of 2015. Sometimes storm chasers provide the only "ground truth" when severe storms strike.

BELOW: Storm chasers and their vehicles head westward out of western Kansas into a complex of severe storms in early May of 2016. Some vehicles are armored for protection against large hail. The storms here will eventually produce a tornado.

Often country roads are limited to packed dirt and gravel, like this one near Protection, Kansas, in late May 2016 with a research group and mobile Doppler radar truck up ahead. If these roads get wet, everyone gets stuck.

Completely flooded roads in Wichita, Kansas, after a storm easily hides roadside ditches, covering them with water, and trapping unsuspecting vehicles. Here is mine as I entered a hotel parking lot late at night in May 2016, being winched out.